Malala Yousafzai
Defender of Education for Girls

Kelly Spence

 Crabtree Publishing Company
www.crabtreebooks.com

REMARKABLE LIVES REVEALED

Author: Kelly Spence

Series research and development:
Reagan Miller

Editorial director: Kathy Middleton

Editor: Crystal Sikkens

Proofreader: Janine Deschenes

Photo researchers: Samara Parent
and Crystal Sikkens

Designer and prepress technician:
Samara Parent

Print coordinator: Katherine Berti

Dedicated by Kelly Spence

For my daughter Hannah, and all little girls who can change the world.

Photographs:
Alamy: ©epa european pressphoto agency b.v.: page 16
AP Photo: ©Bebeto Matthews: page 18; ©Kyodo: page 22
Getty Images: ©Jim Spellman: title page; ©Sean Drakes/CON: pages 4-5, 23; ©OLI SCARFF: page 8;
   ©A MAJEED: page 9; ©Veronique de Viguerie: pages 10, 14, 17; ©AFP: page 11; ©STR: page 13;
   ©Handout: pages 20, 21; ©VEGARD WIVESTAD GROTT: page 25; ©Michael Gottschalk: page 29;
iStockphoto: ©2009 Getty Images: page 15
Keystone: ©Fox Searchlight Pictures: page 28
Photoshot: ©Xinhua: page 19
Shutterstock.com: ©JStone: p 12
Wikimedia Commons: ©Simon Davis/DFID: cover; © W.Kaleem: page 7 (top);
   ©Imranrashid26: page 7 (bottom); ©White House: page 24; ©UK Department for International
   Development: pages 26-27; ©Southbank Centre : page 30 (rop); ©Nicholas Gemini: page 30 (bottom)
All other images from Shutterstock

About the author: Kelly Spence works as a freelance author and editor for educational publishers. She
holds a BA in English and Liberal Arts and a Certificate in Publishing. Kelly lives in the Niagara Region
with her husband, their new baby girl, and a spirited dog named Zoey. She hopes that, like Malala, her
daughter will inspire people to stand up for what they believe in.

Library and Archives Canada Cataloguing in Publication

Spence, Kelly, author
  Malala Yousafzai : defender of education for girls / Kelly Spence.

(Remarkable lives revealed)
Includes index.
Issued in print and electronic format.
ISBN 978-0-7787-2691-3 (hardback).--
ISBN 978-0-7787-2702-6 (paperback) --ISBN 978-1-4271-1812-7 (html)

     1. Yousafzai, Malala, 1997- --Juvenile literature. 2. Girls--
Education--Pakistan--Juvenile literature. 3. Sex discrimination in
education--Pakistan--Juvenile literature. 4. Women social reformers-
-Pakistan--Biography--Juvenile literature. 5. Political activists--
Pakistan--Biography--Juvenile literature. 6. Women Nobel Prize
winners--Pakistan--Biography--Juvenile literature. 7. Girls--Violence
against--Juvenile literature. I. Title.

LC2330.S64 2016   j371.822095491   C2016-904111-5
                                                 C2016-904112-3

Library of Congress Cataloging-in-Publication Data

Names: Spence, Kelly, author.
Title: Malala Yousafzai : defender of education for girls / Kelly Spence.
Description: New York, New York : Crabtree Publishing, [2017] |
  Series:
  Remarkable lives revealed | Includes index.
Identifiers: LCCN 2016026658 (print) | LCCN 2016033883 (ebook) |
  ISBN 9780778726913 (reinforced library binding) |
  ISBN 9780778727026 (pbk.) |
  ISBN 9781427118127 (Electronic HTML)
Subjects: LCSH: Yousafzai, Malala, 1997- | Young women--Education-
  -Pakistan--Biography. | Girls--Education--Pakistan. | Women social
  reformers--Pakistan--Biography. | Social reformers--Pakistan--
  Biography.
Classification: LCC LC2330 .S64 2017 (print) | LCC LC2330 (ebook) |
  DDC 371/.822095491--dc23
LC record available at https://lccn.loc.gov/2016026658

Crabtree Publishing Company
www.crabtreebooks.com   1-800-387-7650

Printed in Canada/082016/TL20160715

**Published
in Canada
Crabtree Publishing**
616 Welland Ave.
St. Catharines, Ontario
L2M 5V6

**Published in
the United States
Crabtree Publishing**
PMB 59051
350 Fifth Ave., 59th Floor
New York, NY 10118

**Published in the
United Kingdom
Crabtree Publishing**
Maritime House
Basin Road North, Hove
BN41 1WR

**Published
in Australia
Crabtree Publishing**
3 Charles Street
Coburg North
VIC, 3058

Contents

Stories to Share

Every person has a unique story to tell. A person's story can be shaped by many things, such as where and when they live. Many stories celebrate people who have done important things or had unique experiences. Other stories are about people who have lived through hard times, such as a war. These stories are sometimes difficult to hear, but are just as important to tell.

What is a Biography?

A biography is the story of a person's life and experiences. We read biographies to learn about another person's life and thoughts. They can be based on many sources of information. Primary sources include a person's own words or pictures. Secondary sources include friends, family, media, and research.

The Right to Learn

It only takes one act of courage to make an ordinary person extraordinary. Many people call Malala Yousafzai (mah-LAH-lah yoo-sahf-ZIGH) remarkable. In 2013, the then 15-year-old **activist** became famous around the world when she was shot in the head for standing up for her **right** to learn. Since then, her story has inspired girls around the world to share their own.

? THINK ABOUT IT

What do you think makes someone remarkable? As you read Malala's story, think about the traits that have made this teen activist so special.

In 2013, Malala wrote a book to share her courageous story with the world.

The Land of Waterfalls

Malala's story begins in the Swat Valley of northwest Pakistan. Like most Pakistani families, the Yousafzais are **Muslim**. In many Muslim homes, the birth of a daughter was not celebrated. The Yousafzai home was different. Malala, who was born on July 12, 1997, in the city of Mingora, was a joy to her family. Her father Ziauddin (ZEE-auh-deen) even added his daughter's name to the family tree. This tradition was usually done for boys only. Malala was the first girl added to her family tree in over 300 years.

> ❝
> *No woman was mentioned. Only men were there. I took the pen, [drew] a line, and [wrote] 'Malala.'*
>
> **—Ziauddin Yousafzai, in *He Named Me Malala***
> ❞

Islam

Muslims follow the Islam (is-LAHM) religion. They believe in one God, called Allah. They follow the teachings of the prophet Muhammad. The Qur'an (koo-RAHN) is the holy book of Islam.

The Strength of a Name

Malala is named after a famous **Pashtun**, Malalai of Maiwand. Maiwand is a city in Afghanistan (af-GAN-uh-stan). There, in the 1800s, Pashtun soldiers were losing a battle against the British. Waving a veil like a flag for the Pashtun soldiers, Malalai, a teenage girl, cried out encouraging words to not give up. She was killed in the battle, but her bravery inspired the army. They gathered their strength and defeated the British. Like Malalai, Malala's bravery has inspired girls to stand up for their right to learn.

Malala grew up listening to her father tell the story of brave Malalai leading the Pashtun soldiers to victory.

The Swat Valley was once a peaceful place, nicknamed "the land of waterfalls."

Like Father, Like Daughter

A few years later, Malala's two brothers, Khushal and Atal, were born. Even with two sons, Ziauddin was close with his daughter. Ziauddin ran a school for girls next door to the family home. He believed an education was important for boys and girls. Ziauddin knew Malala was special. He encouraged his daughter to think for herself and to speak her mind.

Malala was two years old when her brother Khushal (center) was born. Three years later, Atal (second from the left) joined the family.

Pakistani children, including dozens of girls, study during class in Mingora one year after Malala was attacked for standing up for their right to learn.

A Love of Learning

As soon as Malala could walk, she spent much of her time at the school. Going to school was unusual for most girls in Swat. Even Malala's mother, Tor Pekai, was not educated. She spoke only the local Pashtun language, called Pashto (PUHSH-toh). Malala soon learned Pashto as well as **Urdu** (oor-DU) and English. Malala was a good student and enjoyed reading. She felt that books helped her escape the busyness of the outside world. Malala often had the best grades in her class. When she was young, she hoped to become a doctor.

A Dark Shadow over Swat

In 2007, the Taliban (tal-UH-ban) began to gain power in the valley. The Taliban is an **extremist** Islamic group. It interprets the teachings of the Qur'an in ways that differ from most Muslims. Members of the Taliban believe that people who do not follow Islam as they interpret it are their enemies. They do not believe that women should work or go to school. They wanted all women to cover their bodies and dress in **burkas** (BOOR-kuhz) and other traditional Muslim clothing. Soon, the Taliban starting attacking people in the streets and bombing schools throughout the valley.

It was becoming more and more dangerous for girls to go to school. Many students stopped attending classes.

Keeping Watch

Ziauddin feared for the safety of the students attending his school. Malala and her classmates no longer wore their uniforms. Instead they dressed in plain clothes and hid their schoolbags to avoid drawing attention in the streets. Even the sign at the Khushal school was taken down. But still, the Taliban was keeping an eye on the school. One day, a note appeared on the door that read:

> *Sir, the school you are running is **Western** and **infidel**. You teach girls and have a uniform that is un-Islamic. Stop this, or you will be in trouble and your children will weep and cry for you.*
>
> —a note signed by members of the Taliban, noted in *I Am Malala*

In 2008, the Taliban destroyed more than 400 schools in the Swat Valley.

Diary of a Schoolgirl

The Taliban announced that all girls' schools in the valley would close on January 15, 2009. A reporter decided that the world needed to know what was going on in the Swat Valley. He asked Ziauddin to find a student who would share her story. It would be posted online as a **blog** for the BBC, a British news agency. One girl agreed, but her family decided it was too risky to speak out against the Taliban. So, 11-year-old Malala volunteered to take her place.

> ### DO NOT WEAR COLOURFUL DRESSES
> *I was getting ready for school and about to wear my uniform when I remembered that our principal had told us not to wear uniforms and come to school wearing normal clothes instead. So I decided to wear my favourite pink dress. Other girls in school were also wearing colourful dresses. During the morning assembly we were told not to wear colourful clothes as the Taliban would object to it.*
>
> **—Malala's BBC blog post from January 5, 2009**

A Secret Identity

Standing up to the Taliban was dangerous. Malala used a different name to protect her identity. She chose the name Gul Makai, which means "corn flower." Each week, Malala read her diary over the telephone to the reporter. Her stories were then posted in an online blog. The blog ended in March.

? THINK ABOUT IT

A blog can be read by anyone, from anywhere in the world. How did the blog help spread Malala's message about saving girls' schools in Pakistan?

People in the valley feared the Taliban soldiers who controlled the streets and cities with guns and violence.

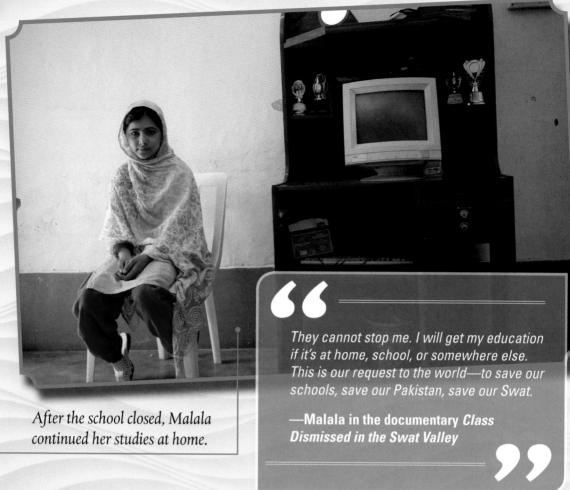

After the school closed, Malala continued her studies at home.

Class Dismissed

While writing the blog, Malala and her family were filmed for a **documentary**. Cameras followed Malala on her last day of classes. She and her friends were angry that the Taliban was in Swat. In the documentary, Malala asked for help to save the school. Because of this her dream of being a doctor had changed. She now wanted to be a **politician**. Then she could make changes that gave all children in Pakistan the right to learn and go to school.

Fleeing in Fear

The Taliban was under pressure by the Pakistan government to lift its ban on girls' education. By the end of February, the Taliban announced that girls could return to school. Few did because of ongoing fear. By May, the Pakistan army had arrived in the valley to fight the Taliban. Malala and her family joined thousands of people fleeing the valley. Her father went to the nearby city of Peshawar (pe-SHAH-wer). The rest of the family stayed with relatives.

School house

After fleeing Swat, Malala soon became homesick. She missed school and her books. When the Pakistan government said it was safe for people to go home, Malala noticed that soldiers had been living in her school.

Trucks and buses filled with people and their belongings carried frightened people away from the violence in the valley.

Gaining Ground

Many people had started to think that Malala might be the girl behind the blog. In December 2009, Ziauddin revealed that his daughter was the real-life Gul Makai. Malala bravely stepped into the spotlight as the voice for girls' education. She spoke up on behalf of girls in all of Pakistan. By then, Malala's message was being heard around the world.

Awards for Peace

In 2011, Malala was nominated for the International Children's Peace Prize. She was also awarded Pakistan's first National Youth Peace Prize. The name of the award was later changed to the National Malala Peace Prize in her honor.

Malala was awarded the National Youth Peace Prize by former prime minister Yousaf Raza Gillani. Afterward Malala gave him a list of things that Pakistan needed, including more schools and a college for girls.

Threatened by the Taliban

Much of the world praised Malala for her courage. But the Taliban did not like the attention she was receiving. They saw her message as a threat to their power. She did not follow their version of Islam. The Taliban began to threaten Malala. They wanted her to stop speaking out for girls' education. Notes were slipped under the door of the family's home. Warnings were also posted on the Internet. But Malala would not stay quiet. The government offered the family protection, but Ziauddin thought it might draw more attention to his daughter. And truly, Malala and her family did not believe the Taliban would harm a child.

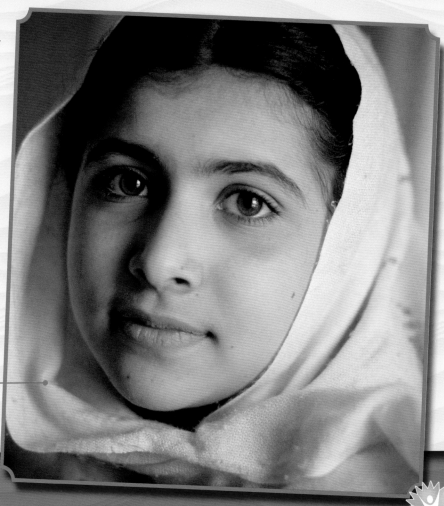

*Malala was not going to let the Taliban stop her from going to school and speaking out about **injustices** in Pakistan.*

Targeted by the Taliban

October 9, 2012, began like most days for Malala. After a late night of studying, she went to write an exam. After the test, she waited with friends for the last bus home. It pulled up and they climbed into the back for the short ride home. Suddenly, the bus pulled over. A masked man with a gun boarded the bus. He wanted to know which girl was Malala. No one spoke, but Malala's classmates looked in her direction. Three shots were fired. One bullet struck Malala. Two others hit her classmates Shazia Ramzan and Kainat Riaz. The gunman fled. The bus driver rushed the three girls to the hospital.

Shazia (left) was struck by a bullet in the hand and shoulder. Kainat (center) was shot in the arm. Today, like Malala, both girls live in England.

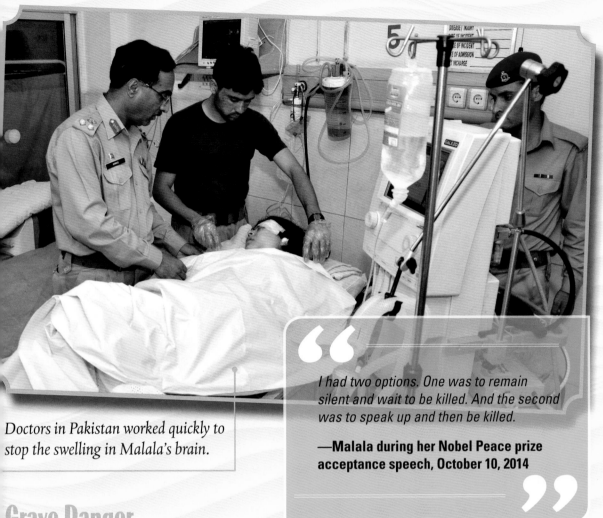

Doctors in Pakistan worked quickly to stop the swelling in Malala's brain.

> I had two options. One was to remain silent and wait to be killed. And the second was to speak up and then be killed.
>
> —Malala during her Nobel Peace prize acceptance speech, October 10, 2014

Grave Danger

Malala was badly hurt. The bullet had struck the top of her head. It went through her neck, then lodged in her back. She was flown by helicopter from the local hospital to an army hospital. The doctors discovered that Malala's brain was swelling. They took out a piece of her skull and placed her in a deep sleep, called a coma. But Malala required more medical care. She was flown to Birmingham, England for treatment.

The Road to Recovery

Malala woke up about a week later. She had few memories of the attack. Malala's road to recovery was long. Several surgeries were needed to repair nerve damage in her face. A metal plate replaced the piece of her skull that had been removed. More surgery was also needed to fix damage to her left ear. Malala spent four months in the hospital. Then her family settled into a new life in England. They all missed Swat. But it was too dangerous for Malala to return to Pakistan.

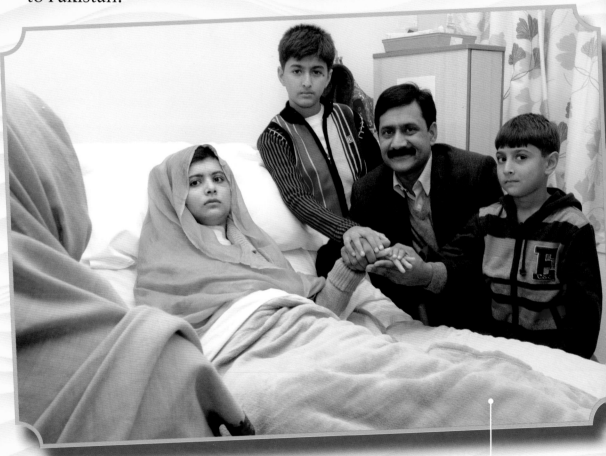

The Yousafzais traveled to England to be with Malala during her recovery. Her father was the first person she asked for when she woke up.

In early 2013, Malala was well enough to leave the hospital to start a new life in England.

The World Reacts

People around the world were shocked when they heard the Taliban had tried to kill a 15-year-old girl. Letters and gifts were mailed to the hospital to support Malala. Over 2 million people signed a **petition** that was sent to the Pakistan government and the United Nations (UN). The petition stated goals they wanted to see met by 2015. This included education for every out-of-school child and making it illegal to **discriminate** against girls.

United Nations

The UN is an organization made up of many countries. They work together to make the world a better place for people everywhere.

Books Instead of Bullets

On her sixteenth birthday, Malala made her first public appearance since the shooting. She traveled to New York City to make a speech at the UN headquarters. About 400 people from over 100 countries gathered to hear her speak. During her speech, she encouraged everyone to make it their own goal to stand up for children's education. At the end of her speech, everyone stood and clapped.

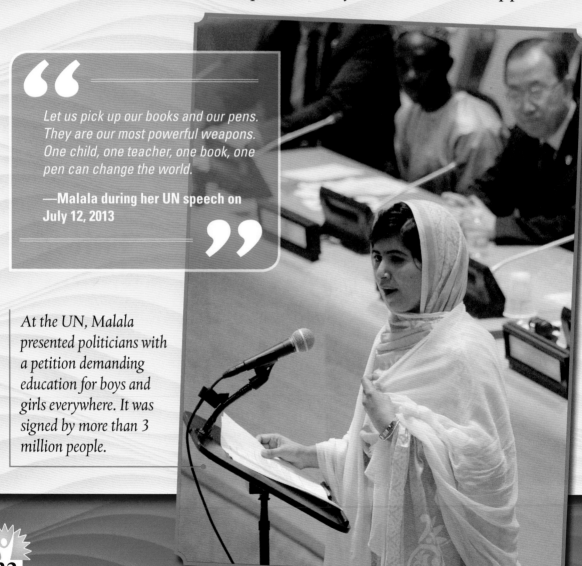

> Let us pick up our books and our pens. They are our most powerful weapons. One child, one teacher, one book, one pen can change the world.
>
> —Malala during her UN speech on July 12, 2013

At the UN, Malala presented politicians with a petition demanding education for boys and girls everywhere. It was signed by more than 3 million people.

Spreading her Message

Malala quickly put her inspiring words into action. She and her father started a charity to organize their efforts. Since 2013, the Malala Fund has worked to educate children in Kenya, Sierra Leone, Nigeria, and Pakistan. It also builds schools for **refugees**.

? THINK ABOUT IT

Malala believes that one individual, even a child, has the power to make change. Why do you think she believes that? What could you do to change something that is important to you?

Malala visits countries around the world to talk about the importance of education. In July 2014, she traveled to Trinidad and Tobago where she met with local schoolchildren.

In November 2013, Malala met with President Barack Obama and his family at the White House.

Making a Difference

Many people, including the queen of England, wanted to meet the young girl leading the movement for girls' education. Every time Malala met a world leader, she asked for their help in putting books in the hands of students in need. Malala brought attention to girls' education everywhere. She also inspired change in her home country. Shortly after the shooting, the Pakistan government passed a new law. It made it illegal for children to not go to school. It also made education free for boys and girls in the whole country.

The Nobel Peace Prize

In 2013, Malala was nominated for the Nobel Peace Prize. This award is given to a person who is working to make the world a better place. In 2014, she was nominated again. That year, at age 17, Malala became the youngest person to ever win the award. She shared the honor with Kailash Satyarthi (KAY-lash sah-tee-AR-tee). He is a children's rights activist from India. Malala used her prize money to help build a high school for girls in Pakistan.

> " I tell my story, not because it is unique, but because it is not. It is the story of many girls...I am Malala. But I am also Shazia. I am Kainat. I am Kainat Soomro. I am Mezon. I am Amina. I am those 66 million girls who are deprived of education. And today I am not raising my voice, it is the voice of those 66 million girls. "
>
> —Malala during her Nobel Peace prize acceptance speech, October 10, 2014

? THINK ABOUT IT

In her Nobel Prize speech, Malala says her story is not unique. She names girls from all over the world who are also fighting for education. How does this help strengthen her message?

Malala and Kailash Satyarthi were each given a gold medal and special diploma at the Nobel Prize ceremony in Oslo, Norway.

The Malala of Syria

Malala has inspired many girls to stand up for education. One of these girls is Syrian activist Muzoon Almellehan (MUH-zoon AL-melh-leh-han). Syria (SEER-ee-uh) has been locked in a **civil war** since 2011. Over 4.8 million people have fled the country. Many live in refugee camps. In 2014, Malala visited one camp near Jordan. There, she met Muzoon. In the camp, many parents wanted their teenage girls to get married to older men. They thought that the husbands would protect their daughters. Muzoon disagreed. She encourages girls to go to school instead of getting married. With an education, Muzoon argues, these girls could take care of themselves.

THINK ABOUT IT

?

Why is it important that children receive an education? How do you think going to school helps girls in countries such as Pakistan and Syria?

Working for Peace

After three years in refugee camps, Muzoon and her family moved to England. Today, Muzoon and Malala are working together to raise money for Syrian children living in the camps. Muzoon plans to someday return to Syria. She wants to use her education to help rebuild the country.

> *We must make a promise to this generation—to empower them with education to rebuild Syria and bring peace.*
>
> **—Malala at the Supporting Syria and the Region conference in London on February 4, 2016**

At the Supporting Syria conference, Malala and Muzoon asked world leaders to commit $1.4 billion to help millions of Syrian children get an education.

Take Action

Malala continues to spread her message on the importance of education around the world. She has even inspired her mother to learn to read and write English. In 2015, on her eighteenth birthday, she opened a school for Syrian refugees in Lebanon. Later that year, she shared her story in a documentary called *He Named Me Malala*.

> *Do not wait for me to do something for your rights. It's your world and you can change it.*
>
> **—Malala during her Nobel Peace prize acceptance speech, October 10, 2014**

From the Director of WAITING FOR SUPERMAN and Academy Award® Winner AN INCONVENIENT TRUTH

HE NAMED ME
MALALA

ONE CHILD, ONE TEACHER, ONE BOOK AND ONE PEN
CAN CHANGE THE WORLD.

He Named Me Malala *has been released in 171 countries and in 45 languages.*

IN THEATRES OCTOBER 2015
www.MALALA.org

The Next Chapter

Still in her teens, Malala's story is only just beginning. Much like her friend Muzoon, she dreams of one day returning to her homeland. But for now it is not safe. The Taliban has said that if she returns, they will try to hurt her again. Malala's bravery and belief in the right for all children to learn continues to inspire people to take a stand for what they believe in. It does not matter where you live, how old you are, or what your story is. It only takes one person to change the world.

One day, Malala wants to become the prime minister of Pakistan.

Writing Prompts

1. How did Malala's childhood impact her later work as an activist?

2. How has Malala's story brought attention to girls' education? Use examples from the text to support your answer.

3. Identify different examples in the story in which Malala showed bravery and determination. What other character traits did she display while spreading her message about girls' education?

Learning More

Books

Langston-George, Rebecca. *For the Right to Learn: Malala Yousafzai's Story*. Mankato. Capstone Young Readers, 2015.

Leggett Abouraya, Karen. *Malala Yousafzai: Warrior with Words*. StarWalk Kids Media, 2014.

McCarney, Rosemary. *Dear Malala, We Stand with You*. Crown Books for Young Readers, 2014.

Wilson, Janet. *Our Rights: How Kids are Changing the World*. Second Story Press, 2013.

Websites

http://mediaroom.scholastic.com/files/JS-102714-Malala.pdf
Read an interview with Malala by Scholastic.

www.malala.org/students
The Malala Fund provides a student toolkit for anyone wishing to join in the fight for girls' education.

www.nobelprize.org/nobel_prizes/peace/laureates/2014/yousafzai-facts.html
Learn about the Nobel Peace Prize, watch Malala's award ceremony, and read Malala and Kailash Satyarthi's stories at this site.

http://community.malala.org/girl-heroes/
Visit the Malala Fund blog to read inspirational stories of girls around the world who, like Malala, have stood up for their right to learn.

Glossary

activist A person who works for social change

blog A website where someone writes their thoughts or experiences

burkas Loose garments that are worn by some Muslim women that cover the face and head

civil war A war fought among people living in the same country

discriminate To treat someone unfairly based on their race, gender, beliefs, or other personal reasons

documentary A movie about a real-life person, event, or issue

extremist A person or group that has extreme viewpoints and are often violent

infidel Someone who acts in ways that are in opposition to a specific religion

injustices Unfair treatments

Muslim A follower of Islam

Pashtun A group of people who live in Afghanistan and Pakistan

petition A written request given to someone, usually supported by individual signatures

politician An elected person who is involved in the government

prophet A person who shares religious messages from a God

refugees People who have fled their country due to religious or political persecution

right Something that everyone is entitled to, regardless of their gender, ethnicity, or religion

traits Qualities that stand out about a person or group of people

Urdu One of Pakistan's official languages, largely spoken by Muslims

Western Describing ideas and the lifestyles found in North America and western Europe

Index

746.434   Robertson, Rhoda.
ROBERTSON   Romantic crochet.